Embroidery

A beginner's step-by-step guide to stitches and techniques

CHARLOTTE GERLINGS

Design Originals

an Imprint of Fox Chapel Publishing

www.d-originals.com

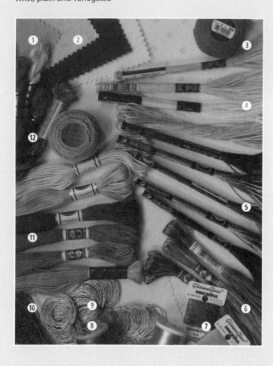

Materials provided and photographed by kind permission of DMC Creative World Ltd (visit www.dmccreative.co.uk to find out more), and Madeira UK (www.madeira.co.uk)

To Thelma M. Nye, craft editor at B.T. Batsford Ltd for over thirty years and friend and advisor to many grateful authors and designers.
And with thanks to Professor Anne Morrell, author of numerous books and articles on embroidery, for her generous advice and input on this title.

Charlotte Gerlings was born into a home where dressmaking and creating stage costumes were everyday activities. She has an MA in Fine Art from Wimbledon School of Art and has written books on art history and crafts.

Illustrated by David Woodroffe
Peacock cushion project devised by Divya Lahoria, with inspiration from The Techniques of Indian Embroidery by Anne Morrell

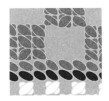

CONTENTS

Introduction 4

PART I: EQUIPMENT AND MATERIALS

Needles 5
Basic equipment 6
Working with hoops and frames 7
Fabric 8
Threads 10

PART II: HAND EMBROIDERY METHODS AND TECHNIQUES

Transferring your design 11
Preparing fabric 12
Preparing threads 13
Starting and fastening off 14
Stitch directory 15
A Back stitch alphabet 30

PART III: MACHINE EMBROIDERY METHODS AND TECHNIQUES

The sewing machine 31
Using hoops and stabilizers 34
Techniques to try 35
Two special effects 36
Motifs 37
PROJECT: Bag keeper 38

PART IV: REGIONAL EMBROIDERY

The Indian tradition 39
PROJECT: Peacock cushion cover 42
The Peruvian Paracas 43
European folk embroidery 44

Washing and mounting 46
Glossary 47
Index of stitches 48

INTRODUCTION

Different writers have attempted to define "embroidery." Most commonly, it is described as "thread worked on an existing fabric by hand or machine." Sometimes, embroidery is referred to as "needlework" or the embellishment of fabric, enriching it with needle and thread.

Hand stitches have been around for as long as there have been needles, and hand embroidery for as long as people wanted to decorate woven fabric, felt or leather. Embroidery stitches come from very different origins. Some undoubtedly have their foundation in early textiles, basketry, mat-making and weaving; others have developed from early sewing. It is not surprising, then, that there is a wide range of names for them and this can cause confusion.

Stitches are produced by a needle and thread being inserted and brought out through the fabric at specific intervals. This action, the repetition of actions, and grouping of threads, produces an endless variety of surfaces and combinations of effects. Today, embroidery can be used in many ways and for outcomes that are practical or ornamental, as well as those that express a concept and have no practical application.

Like workers in other arts and crafts, you have to make a start somewhere and I am sure that once you allow the stitches to be used in a way that pleases you, you will be bitten by the bug and want to continue learning and expressing ideas, patterns, whatever, using the marks that embroidery stitches can make.

You don't have to know or use a large number of stitches to make embroidery. However, you do need a needle, thread and fabric that are sympathetic, one to the other. There is nothing more frustrating than tugging your thread through a fabric because you have the wrong materials. Get that right before you start. Stitch away from or towards yourself – people do stitch in different directions, left- or right-handed – you will discover what is most comfortable for you.

In 1936, a really far-sighted teacher called Rebecca Crompton wrote, "...A teacher of embroidery need not teach too many stitches at once – although they may all have to be learnt eventually. A doctor may intend that a bottle of medicine should be taken, but not all at once."

So, be patient and true to what you like. It's fine to make large rough stitches or small precious ones, there is no right or wrong way to use them – but you may have to practice with different fabrics and threads to achieve the desired effect.

If you have no idea where to start then perhaps you could look at Indian embroidery. Some of the most wonderful embroidery is still made in India and you can find many examples in shops and museum collections.

Anne Morrell

Professor Anne Morrell was formerly principal lecturer at Manchester Metropolitan University Department of Textiles/Fashion, which has the only embroidery degree course in the UK. She is currently consultant to the Ahmedabad Calico Museum in Gujarat, India, where she visits each year, systematically recording and documenting traditional Indian textile techniques.

PART ONE:
EQUIPMENT AND MATERIALS

NEEDLES

Needles are manufactured in a wide range of lengths and thicknesses; the higher the number, the finer the needle. Take care to select the right size and type of needle for the thread and fabric you are using.

1 **Sharps** Medium-length and pointed, with a round eye, for general sewing with cotton or polyester thread.

2 **Crewel or embroidery** Pointed like sharps, but with a long oval eye like a tapestry needle, for thicker or multiple threads.

3 **Tapestry** Blunt-tipped with a long oval eye, used in counted thread embroidery.

4 **Betweens** Short and sharp, with a small round eye. Used for fine stitching and quilting.

5 **Milliner's or straws** Very long and thin with a round eye, used for applying decoration.

6 **Bodkin** Thick, blunt-tipped, with an eye large enough to carry cord, elastic or ribbon through loops and casings.

7 **Glover's or leather** Has a sharp 3-sided tip for piercing leather and PVC without tearing.

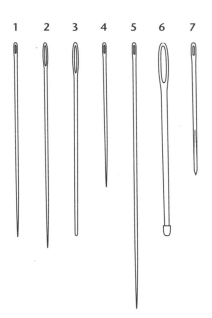

Needle eyes

Needle eyes are either round or oval; round ones are the smallest and long oval the largest. Although a small needle helps with fine work, if the eye is too tight around the thread or yarn, it will be difficult to pull through the fabric and could fray the thread in the process.

Most needles are nickel plated, though the quality varies. They sometimes become discolored and may mark your work if left in the fabric; put them away when you have finished. Some people keep a tiny cushion packed firmly with emery powder, which is a useful abrasive for cleaning needles and pins. Gold- and platinum-plated needles will not discolor or rust but are more expensive.

BASIC EQUIPMENT

A **Needles, pins and pincushion**

B **Thimble**

C **Seam ripper**

D **Dressmaking shears**

E **Scissors**

F **Embroidery scissors**

G **Iron**

H **Sewing machine**

I **Embroidery threads**

J **Laying tool:** a small pointed stick of metal or wood for smoothing and straightening embroidery threads as you stitch (a yarn darner will do as well)

K **Masking tape**

L **Embroiderers' transfer pencil**

M **Fabric marking pencil**

N **Magnifying lamp**

O **Graph paper for charting designs**

P **Dressmakers' carbon paper**

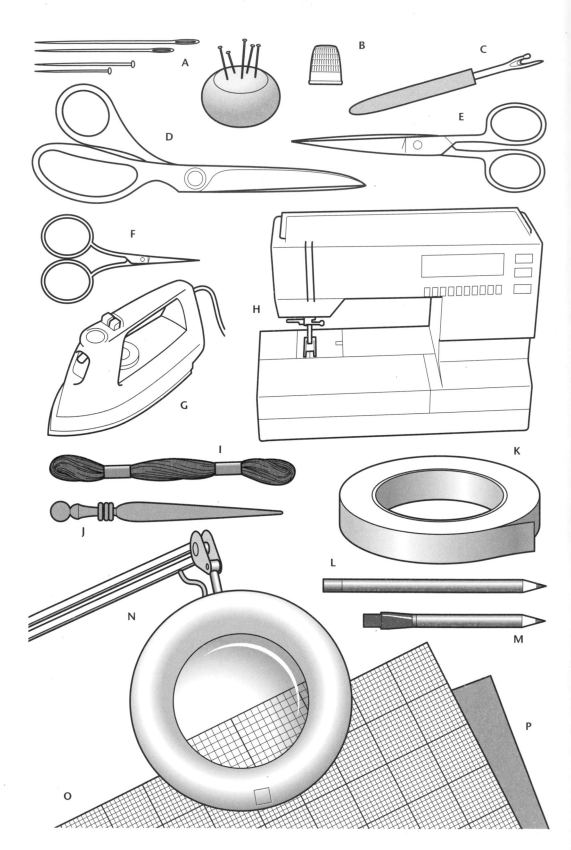

WORKING WITH HOOPS AND FRAMES

Hoops and frames are not essential equipment – many embroiderers prefer to work "in hand" – but progress is generally quicker and more accurate when the ground fabric is evenly stretched and supported.

Hoops and frames

A standard embroidery hoop (A), also known as a tambour (pp. 34 and 39), consists of an inner and outer ring of wood or plastic. The fabric is first placed over the inner ring and the outer one is fastened around both by tightening the metal screw.

Avoid hoop marks on your fabric by first wrapping both rings with bias binding or placing tissue paper between the outer ring and the embroidery (tear the tissue away from the stitching area). Remove the hoop when you are not working.

A hoop or frame (B) of any size can be mounted on a stand (C and D) or in a clamp (E), leaving both hands free for stitching. Many people find that stabbing the needle up and down through the fabric, with one hand above and one below, is comfortable and helps to reduce any pain or cramping of the hands and wrists.

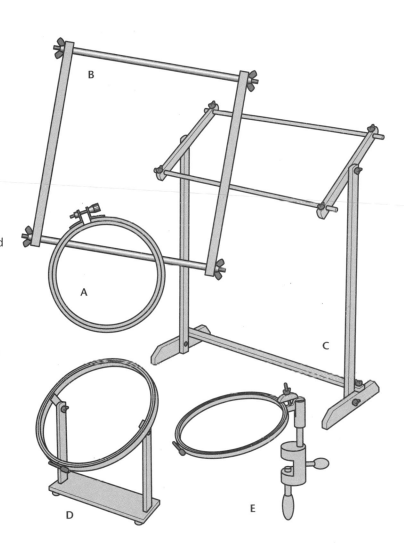

Slate frame

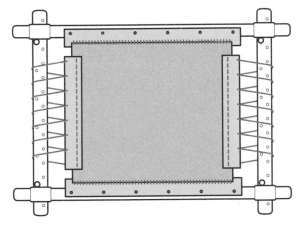

Despite its name, a 'slate' frame is made from wood. First stitch your fabric top and bottom to the strips of tape attached to the rollers. Roll any excess fabric around one roller before slotting on and pegging the two flat sides to complete the frame. Stretch the fabric tight and sew a strip of tape down both sides. With a curved needle and strong thread, lace the fabric evenly over each side of the frame, tighten, and secure firmly at the ends.

FABRIC

The background texture and color of your fabric is important. Modern fabrics consist of natural or man-made fibers, often mixed to combine their best qualities.

Crewel cockatrice

Crewel embroidery was traditionally worked in wool on linen twill fabric. This 17th century cockatrice would have formed part of the densely stitched decoration for some elaborate bed hangings. Twill is substantial and makes a fine, long-lasting upholstery fabric.

Woven fabric

Every woven fabric belongs to one of three types:

Plain weave   Alternate warp (lengthwise) threads go over one and under one of the weft (crosswise) threads. Linen, poplin, muslin, and organza are familiar examples.

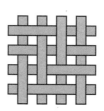

Twill weave   Interlaces warp and weft threads over and under two or more threads progressively, to produce a clear diagonal pattern on hardwearing fabrics like denim or gabardine.

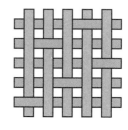

Satin weave   A smooth, glossy, compact surface created by long silky "floats" that leave no weft visible; the reverse is matt.

The grain

The grain of a fabric is the direction in which the warp and weft threads lie. The warp runs lengthwise, parallel to the selvage: this is the *lengthwise grain*. The weft follows the *crosswise grain*, at right angles to the selvage.

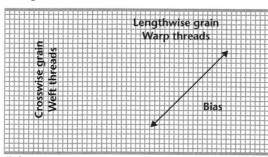

The bias

The bias lies along any diagonal line between the lengthwise and crosswise grains. True bias is at the 45-degree angle where you will get the maximum stretch. Bias strips are often used for piping and binding edges because of their flexibility on curves and corners.

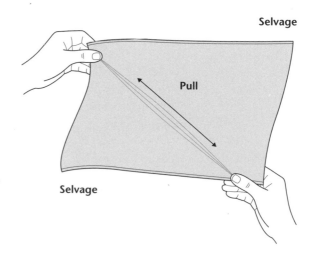

Counted thread fabrics

The two most widely used fabrics for counted cross stitch come in a range of neutral tones and colors.

Aida

This block weave fabric is favored by beginners because of its regular construction and visible stitch holes. It also has a stiffer finish for hand-held work. It is worth noting that unworked areas have a very distinct texture compared with evenweave, so be sure this is the effect you want.

Evenweave and aida are interchangeable with the aid of a little math. So, if a pattern calls for 28-count evenweave stitched over 2 threads of the fabric, use a 14-count aida and stitch into every hole instead. In the same way, you would replace 32-count evenweave with 16-count aida, and 22-count with 11-count.

Evenweave

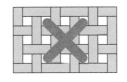

An evenweave is any natural or manmade fabric having the same number of threads per inch (2.5 cm) counted vertically and horizontally; this keeps the cross stitches square and even.
It is frequently made of either linen or cotton.

Evenweave threads are usually of uniform thickness, though the pure linens are slightly less regular. Cross stitch is worked over two threads, so you will stitch into alternate holes. The greater the thread count per inch, sometimes given as HPI (holes per inch), the finer the cloth and the smaller your stitches will be.

Luxury fabrics

The sumptuous clothing of the Byzantines (395–1453 CE) frequently employed the art of the embroiderer. They were especially fond of geometric patterns, also flowers and leaves, often incorporating birds or mythological creatures. Many types of thread were used, including gold, and silk in vivid reds, blues, purples, and yellows.

The Byzantine influence extended west and north throughout the Middle Ages (c. 500–c. 1500 CE). The highly prized medieval English embroidery called Opus Angelicanum was worked in gold thread on velvet or silk twill, and traded all across Europe. It was acquired by royalty and by the Church for ecclesiastical vestments.

> The tighter the weave, the less likely a fabric is to shrink during or after manufacture. The store label will say if a fabric is pre-shrunk. If not, and if necessary, shrink it yourself before use. Wash and dry according to the care label, which will also reveal whether the fabric is colorfast.

THREADS

Embroidery threads can be bought in balls, on spools, or in skeins and hanks (see the selection on the rear cover and key information on p. 2). The shawl border below was worked in silver and gold but there is no reason why embroiderers shouldn't try anything from ribbon to string or fine wire.

Choose threads in natural light if possible because artificial lighting intensifies certain colors and dulls others. The fibers that you choose are important for the texture or finish of your embroidery and always bear in mind the end use of whatever you make. Do not buy cheap machine thread – it breaks easily and may not perform very smoothly. It could also shrink or run in the wash.

Stranded cotton [floss] Often called "silk" and the most commonly used embroidery thread. It consists of six divisible strands and is packaged in a small skein.

Perle [pearl] cotton Shiny 2-ply twisted thread. Unlike stranded cotton, it cannot be separated into strands. However, it is available in various thicknesses.

Soft cotton Thick, stranded cotton, unmercerized, with a matt finish. Ideal for novices working on the 6-count (six holes per inch) block-weave fabric known as "Binca".

Stranded rayon High-gloss six-stranded thread [floss].

Z-twist rayon Glossy 4-ply twist, spun clockwise.

Metallic threads A wide category; metallics are slightly abrasive with a tendency to fray at the ends. Use a large-eyed needle to make a bigger hole in the cloth and reduce the drag on both thread and fabric. For this reason it is best to work with short lengths.

Blending filament Very fine metallic thread for blending with others in the same needle, to create special effects (p. 13).

Space-dyed (or variegated) threads Factory-dyed in multiple colors, or in shades of a single color, at regular intervals along the thread.

Hand-dyed threads Dyed by hand using one or more colors, possibly neither light- nor color-fast.

Machine embroidery threads Available in plain and variegated colors like those for hand embroidery. Most threads are numbered from 100 to 12, where the larger number means a finer thread. If using a digitized embroidery pattern, load up with a size 40 thread. Those thicker than size 30 are generally too heavy for most embroidery designs. Shiny machine threads add luster to close stitching such as satin stitch. Their softness and pliability work well for free-motion stitching.

Cotton machine embroidery thread Usually size 50 but the matt finish gives it a thicker appearance.

Polyester machine embroidery thread Colorfast and durable. Compatible with rayon so they may be run together.

Rayon machine embroidery thread Tends to slip so it is advisable to wind the bobbin with matching cotton or polyester thread and keep the shiny rayon for the top surface of your piece. Rayon dyes can fade with strong sunlight or frequent washing.

Silk Obtainable on spools for machine sewing. Check whether it is washable or dry-clean only.

You can buy shade cards, including actual thread samples, from major manufacturers such as DMC, Anchor, Coats, Madeira and Kreinik and they are obtainable from online needlecraft suppliers. Software is also available to provide accurate color matching across the different thread brands.

PART TWO:

HAND EMBROIDERY METHODS AND TECHNIQUES

TRANSFERRING YOUR DESIGN

Here are three standard techniques for transferring a design onto fabric.

Scaling a design

(Reverse the size order below to make the image larger)

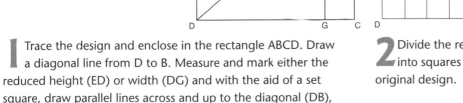

1 Trace the design and enclose in the rectangle ABCD. Draw a diagonal line from D to B. Measure and mark either the reduced height (ED) or width (DG) and with the aid of a set square, draw parallel lines across and up to the diagonal (DB), to meet at point F.

2 Divide the rectangle ABCD into squares across the original design.

3 Rule up a smaller sheet, the same size as EFGD, into the same number of divisions and copy the original, square by square until the reduced design is complete.

Tracing with carbon paper

Draw or trace a design onto thin paper. Place a sheet of dressmakers' carbon paper face down on RS of fabric (use a light color for dark fabric and vice versa). Place design on top, and pin all three together. Draw firmly over design once more to transfer image onto fabric.

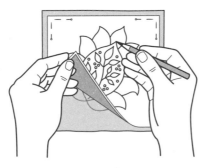

Hot-iron transfer

Draw a design on tracing paper. Turn it over and trace reversed image with an embroiderers' transfer pencil. With transfer side down, pin paper to RS of fabric. Press down directly onto paper with low-heat iron for a few seconds. Do not drag or image may smudge.

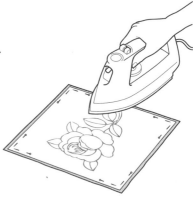

PREPARING FABRIC

Almost any fabric can be embroidered, from finest silk organza to felt or leather. Whether working in the hand or on a frame, the fabric has first to be prepared; for example, by pressing out creases, cutting away the selvage, or maybe dyeing or color spraying.

Sometimes the ground fabric is used alone, and sometimes a backing of mull (stiff muslin) or fine cotton is tacked [basted] on for strength. A very small or irregular shape can be tacked onto a larger piece for ease of working. Cut a hole into the supporting fabric on the wrong side so the embroidery is made on the top layer only. For use of stabilizers, see p. 34.

Four ways of keeping raw edges neat

With 3 and 4, be aware that you will have to cut away ½ in [1 cm] all round afterwards. Chemicals and adhesives will damage the fabric in the long run.

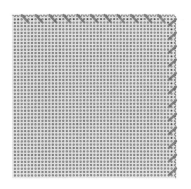

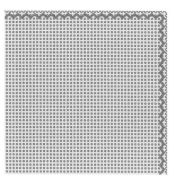

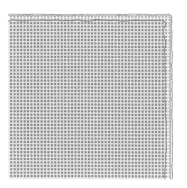

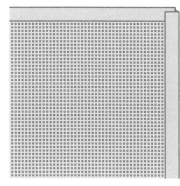

1 Overstitch round the edges by hand with sewing cotton, or roll a small hem if you wish.

2 Zigzag stitch round the edges with a sewing machine.

3 Apply an anti-fray fluid sparingly and allow to dry before working.

4 Frame with masking tape.

Thread organizer You might like to make an organizer for use during your project. Cut one thread of each color to a working length (about 18 in [45 cm]) and loop it through a card with the corresponding number of holes punched down one side, where it remains ready for the needle. With the project name at the top and the manufacturer's shade number beside each hole, you will also have a handy record card when finished.

Metallic threads tend to twist or break more easily, so it is advisable to cut those into shorter lengths (about 12 in [30 cm]). They also tend to unravel at the ends, which can be stopped with anti-fray fluid. Ends can be prepared in advance on the thread organizer and eventually trimmed off.

PREPARING THREADS

How many strands to use

As a rule, the number of strands of cotton [floss] that you sew with generally matches the thickness of one thread pulled out from the edge of the ground fabric.

Separating and recombining stranded cotton [floss]

Multiple strands of cotton [floss] used straight from the skein can produce bumpy stitches, so it is worth taking the trouble to separate the strands, smooth them straight and put them together again in the same direction. This will reduce twisting and tangling, and the stitches will lie better.

Grip one strand firmly at the top and draw your other hand down taking the remaining threads with you until the single strand is free. The others will bunch up but won't become knotted. Finally, lay all the strands out straight and reassemble them as you wish.

Tweeding

Different colored strands threaded into the same needle is known as tweeding. Achieved by separating strands (see above), it is a good way of introducing textural effects and also of creating extra colors without buying more; for instance, blue and pink strands will produce mauve. There is also a very fine metallic thread known as a blending filament designed for combination with ordinary stranded cotton [floss].

The blending filament and stranded cotton [floss] will not slip when the filament is threaded up as shown. The cotton is threaded up afterwards in the usual way.

Single strand outline

Many pictorial cross stitch designs are outlined in back stitch. This is often sewn in black with just one or two strands of cotton [floss].

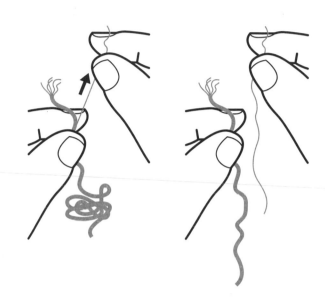

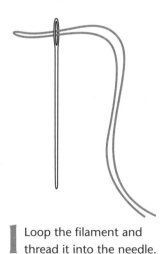

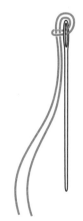

1 Loop the filament and thread it into the needle.

2 Thread the free ends through the loop.

3 Pull the ends of the filament very gently to secure it in the eye of the needle.

STARTING AND FASTENING OFF

No knots

Knots at the back will appear as unsightly bumps on the front of your work when it is finally pressed and mounted. They will even pop right through the weave if it is loose enough. So, when starting out, push your needle through from the wrong side leaving a 1½ in [3 cm] tail of thread at the back. Hold the tail against the fabric as you go and it will soon be caught down by the new stitches.

The correct way to fasten off is to run the thread under three or four wrong-side stitches, either horizontally or vertically. Whipping the end around one of those stitches helps to secure it.

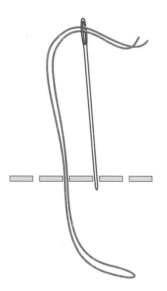

Waste knots

First knot the end of the thread and from the right side push your needle through to the back, leaving the knot on the surface of the fabric. Next, bring your needle through again about 1 in [2.5 cm] from the knot and start

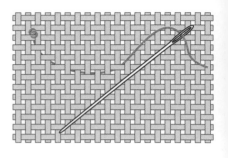

stitching towards it. Stab stitch steadily and be sure of completely covering the thread at the back. When that is done, trim the knot from the front.

An away waste knot is placed well away from the stitching and is not covered by it. When cut off, it leaves a longer tail at the back, which is threaded into a needle and woven in.

The loop start or lark's head knot

Two conditions hold for this method: first, working with an even number of strands of cotton [floss]; and second, the working length of thread should be doubled to 36 in [90 cm].

Separate one strand of cotton [floss] if you are stitching with two strands (two for four, and three for six). Fold the strand(s) double and thread the loose ends into your needle.

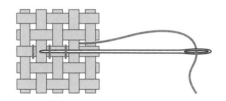

1 Stab the needle up through the fabric from the wrong to the right side and pull enough thread with it to leave a small loop at the back.

2 Make your first stitch and, with the needle back on the wrong side, pass it through the waiting loop.

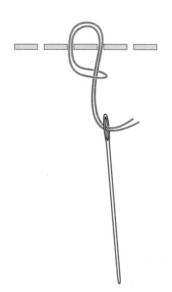

3 As you pull the thread it will draw the loop neatly against the fabric.

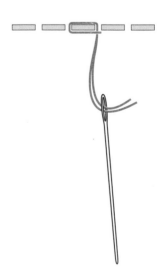

STITCH DIRECTORY

The stitches in this directory are arranged in "families," which makes for interesting comparisons and possibilities. See p. 48 for an alphabetical list. The illustrations show when the needle actually goes in and out of the fabric and when it passes behind a part of the stitch being made without piercing the fabric.

KNOTTED STITCHES

French knot

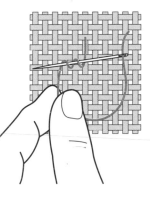

1 Wrap thread twice around the needle and pull gently to tighten coils towards the tip.

2 Insert needle, press thumb down to hold coils and pull thread gently but firmly through fabric, leaving a perfect knot on the surface.

Bullion knot

Use a straight needle with a narrow eye so the thread passes as smoothly as possible through the coils. Hold coils with thumb until needle and thread are through. Turn to complete stitch and tighten carefully.

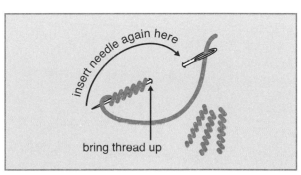

insert needle again here

bring thread up

Four-legged knot

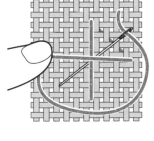

1 Make a vertical stitch and hold the thread across halfway point while sliding needle down diagonally from right to left. Thread hangs in a loop below the vertical.

2 Pull needle and thread carefully through loop to form a knot around the center. Take needle left, level with knot, and insert to complete cross.

Knotted stitch

Make a single diagonal stitch, perform a double loop over and insert needle immediately below. Pull through to form knot.

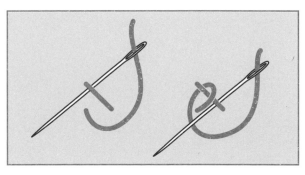

RUNNING AND BACK STITCHES

Running stitch

Secure thread with two small stitches. With needle at front, push into fabric and out again in one move. Stitch and space should be of equal length. Fasten off with a back stitch.

Back stitch

Begin exactly as for running stitch then stitch back over the first space. Needle out again at one stitch space ahead of the last stitch made. Repeat with needle back in again at the point where the previous stitch ended.

Double running (Holbein) stitch

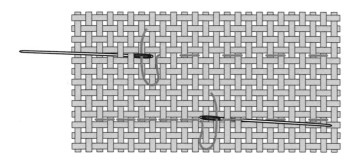

Looks like back stitch but actually consists of two passes of running stitch, where the second pass returns and precisely fills the gaps left by the first. Done with precision, this makes a far neater underside than that of back stitch. Ideal for unlined items such as bookmarks.

Double running steps

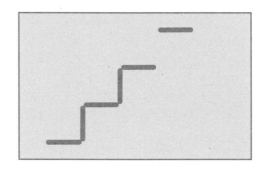

Stepped stitches constructed in two passes. Here vertical running stitches fill the gaps between the horizontal ones. Stitches must be of equal length and at perfect right-angles to each another.

Dog-tooth (Bosnian) stitch

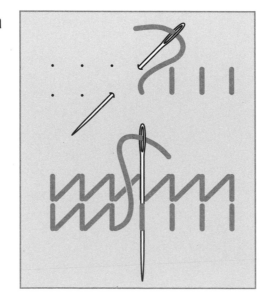

Worked in a similar way to double running. Oblique stitches return along a line of evenly spaced verticals. Also suitable for counted thread work.

Threaded running stitch

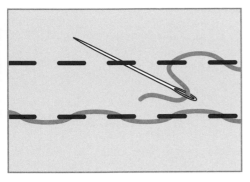

Slide the needle up and down through the line of running stitch, without piercing the fabric until the end. Finish off on the wrong side. Looks most effective when a second color is used for the threading.

Whipped running stitch

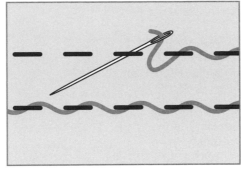

Another effective use of a second color. Whip by sliding the needle through each running stitch in one direction only. Like threaded running, this is done without piercing the fabric until the end. Finish off on the wrong side.

Double threaded back stitch

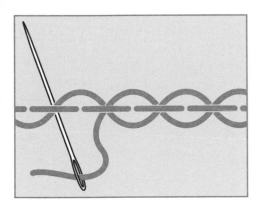

Double threading produces a heavy line. Slide the needle up and down through the stitches, without piercing the fabric until the end. Finish off on the wrong side. Repeat until the stitches are completely threaded above and below.

Pekinese stitch

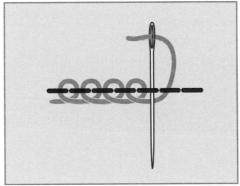

First work a line of small back stitches then loop the second thread through the stitches without piercing the fabric. The second thread travels forward two stitches and back one with each complete threading action.

Trellis back stitch

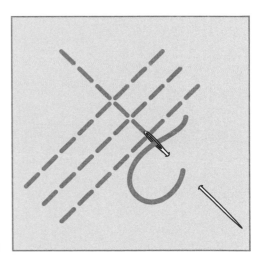

This is a diagonal arrangement of back stitched lines. The ends of the stitches should meet.

STRAIGHT AND CROSS STITCHES

Speckling

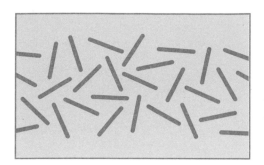

Quite small, straight stitches made in different directions and evenly distributed. This is a useful filling stitch for providing texture to a particular area.

Arrowhead stitch

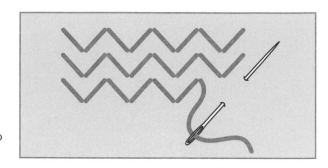

Worked vertically or horizontally, the stitches should always be at right-angles to each other. Combines well with other stitches and is also suitable for counted thread work.

Fern stitch

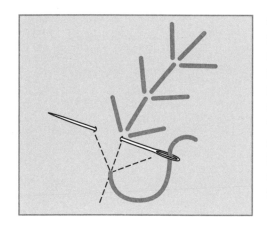

Consists of three parts, which may either be all the same length (as shown) or stitched so that the "branches" form a leaf shape. In its linear form, fern is a decorative means of fastening appliqué.

Fishbone stitch

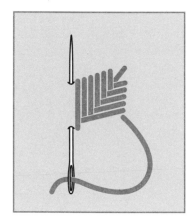

Close-woven stitches are worked from the outer edge in to a central line where they overlap.

Sheaf stitch (single)

Suitable for counted thread work. Work three straight stitches vertically or horizontally. Bring needle up halfway and pass twice around all three stitches without piercing the fabric, tighten and insert a second time alongside the first.

Cross stitch

Cross stitch is worked by the counted thread method on an evenly woven fabric (p. 9). The most important rule about cross stitch is that all the top stitches go in one direction for a uniform appearance.

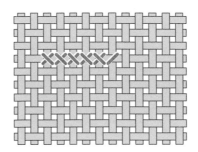

The traditional English method completes each X before moving on to the next.

The Danish method stitches one leg of the Xs first, and completes them on a return pass.

Smyrna (double cross) stitch

Using the counted thread method, one cross stitch has another cross worked vertically over it. Follow the numbered points.

Boxed cross stitch

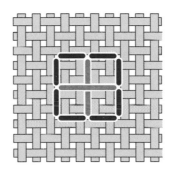

Using the counted thread method, work a vertical cross stitch. Box in with a square formation of back stitches or double running.

Woven (braided) cross

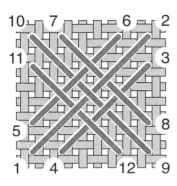

Using the counted thread method, follow the numbered points, weaving the final 3 stitches in and out of the first set.

Algerian eye stitch

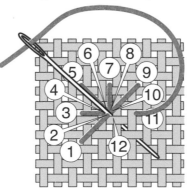

1 Bring needle through at left base and work 8 straight stitches clockwise into the same central hole, following the numbered points.

2 Pull stitches firmly to create the central hole. Do not allow threads on wrong side to cover it.

Long-armed cross stitch

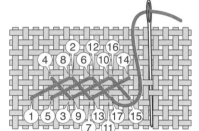

1 Following the numbers, stitch a long diagonal right. Needle in at top and out directly below. Cross over previous stitch. Needle in at top and out again below.

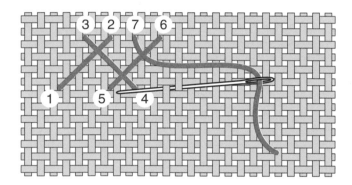

2 Repeat to form a row, following the numbered points. Repeated rows make a bold background filling.

Rice stitch

1 Work a row of counted cross stitch on an evenly woven fabric.

2 In a second color and with finer thread, work a back stitch over each half leg of each cross stitch to form the characteristic diamond shapes.

HERRINGBONE STITCHES

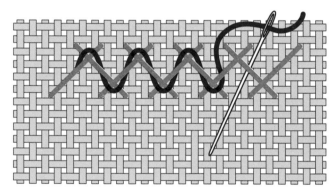

Basic herringbone Stitch a long diagonal from left to right. Insert needle at top and bring out left. Crossing the previous stitch, make another diagonal right and down. Needle in at base and out left. Repeat to form a row, following the numbered points.

Threaded herringbone stitch

Work a row of herringbone stitch. Secure second color thread on wrong side by whipping round existing stitches. Bring needle through and weave in and out of herringbone without piercing the fabric. Needle in and fasten off on wrong side.

Tied herringbone stitch

Work a zigzag line of coral stitch (p. 24) over a foundation of herringbone.

STEM, SPLIT, FLY AND FEATHER STITCHES

Stem stitch

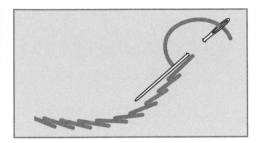
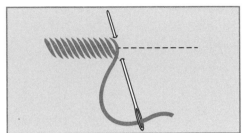

1 To follow curves or straight lines, work slanted back stitch with the needle coming out a little above the previous stitch.

2 Create a thicker, more rope-like effect by inserting the needle at a sharper angle and increasing the number of strands of thread.

Raised band stem stitch

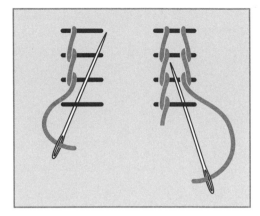

Begin working stem stitch over a series of foundation bars without piercing the fabric (left). Work symmetrically from each side inward (right). Use as a single band or as a filler.

Split stitch

A small, delicate line stitch usually worked with silk in a frame. The needle pierces the working thread each time.

Fly stitch

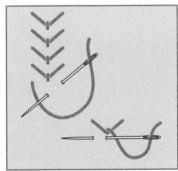

Starting left, a loop hangs between two higher points while the needle emerges at the center below. Hold the loop flat with the thumb (left). A small stitch ties the loop and another stitch starts left (right). The tie can be any length and the entire stitch combines readily to form borders and allover patterns.

Feather stitch

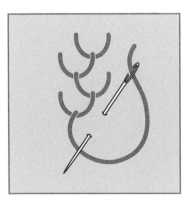

Stitch alternately to left and right. Always slant the needle in toward the center while holding the thread down with the thumb.

Double feather stitch

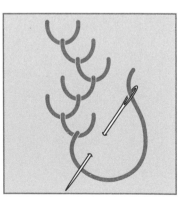

Similar to single feather stitch, with two additional stitches worked either side of the stitch line.

CHAIN STITCHES

Chain stitch

A looped stitch that works both as outline and filling. Constructs well with three or more strands of embroidery cotton [floss].

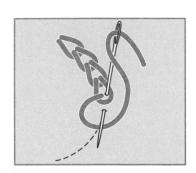

Bring needle through and insert again beside exit hole, leaving a loop on top. Bring needle up again through the loop, below the starting point. Pull gently until loop forms a rounded link. Repeat.

Detached chain (daisy) stitch

A quick stitch for depicting flowers and leaves, this variation on the chain loop can be made to form a circle of as many petals as you wish.

1 Begin as for chain stitch but work only one loop.

2 Make a small tying stitch to hold loop at its widest point. Needle through again at start of next petal.

A delicate Edwardian design for embroidery with daisy stitch and stem or split stitch. Ideal for use on a table or bed linen project, either as a single-unit corner-piece or linked in a ring.

Checkered chain

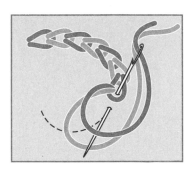

Thread needle with two colors and work alternate chain stitches with them. Take care to keep the unused thread above the needle point.

Tête de boeuf

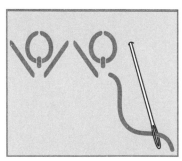

A detached chain stitch is set between two small straight stitches made in a V shape.

Broad chain

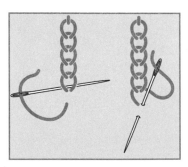

Reversed chain stitch, best worked fairly small. Start with a vertical running stitch. Pass needle back through it without piercing the fabric (left). Form chain link by taking stitch in fabric (right) and repeat.

Open chain

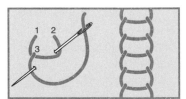

Keep needle slanted (left). The more horizontal it is, the wider and shallower the chain link (right). Stitch benefits from added ornamentation.

Back-stitched chain

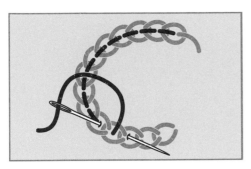

Make a foundation chain. Using a different-colored thread if desired, needle up at center of second chain stitch and back down into the first, coming up again through the third.

Whipped chain

When the second thread is whipped over the total width and pulled tightly, the chain resembles a cord.

Raised band chain stitch

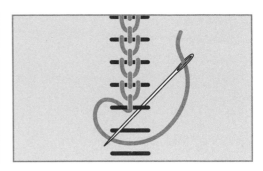

Worked over a foundation of closely spaced straight stitches, the chain stitch completes the band without piercing the fabric.

Coral zigzag stitch

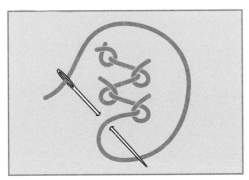

Working from left to right between two parallel lines (drawn or tacked [basted]), make the first loop left like a chain stitch with crossed arms. Bring needle out through the loop, pull to form a knot and repeat to the right. These stitches should be worked close together.

Slipped chain stitch

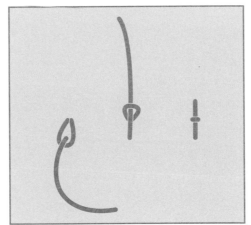

Make a single chain (left) but instead of a tying stitch, pull the thread in the opposite direction (center), simultaneously tightening the loop to a small flat tie. Needle in to complete (right). Often used to highlight an outline.

Wheatear stitch

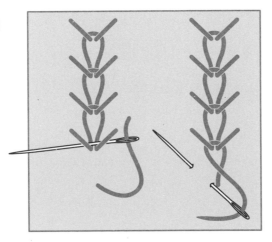

Draw or tack [baste] a vertical line for guidance and make two straight stitches inward, forming a right-angled V. Needle out again on the line, about ¼ in [6 mm] below. Slide needle through V without piercing the fabric (left). Needle in again to make a loop and out again ready to repeat (right).

BUTTONHOLE STITCHES AND SCROLL STITCH

Blanket stitch

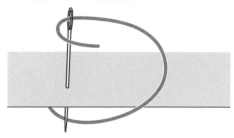

1 Secure thread on WS and bring through at fabric edge. Needle in at desired stitch height and width to the right. Needle out again directly below.

2 Pass the needle forward through the loop, forming a half-hitch, and tighten the thread against the fabric edge. Repeat to form a row.

Buttonhole stitch

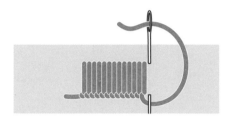

With the same basic construction as blanket stitch, this stitch evolved to seal the raw edges of a buttonhole. Stitched closely like satin stitch (p. 26), it can be used to neaten both straight and curved edges and features in cutwork embroidery like broderie anglaise (p. 36).

Coral stitch

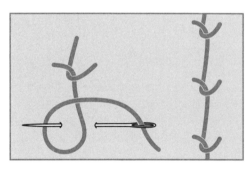

Hold thread taut and push needle in and out of the fabric either side of the thread (left). Pull through the resulting loop until a knot is formed. Repeat at regular intervals (right), either in straight lines or curved.

Wheel buttonhole (ring)

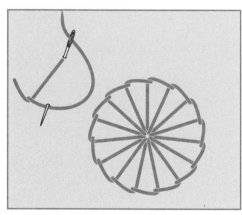

Work buttonhole stitch in a circle on a firmly woven fabric.

Scroll

Make a loop to the right and take a tiny vertical stitch within it. Pull thread through to complete the scroll. Make another loop to the right and repeat in a straight line. Looks better in twisted rather than stranded thread.

Double buttonholed bar

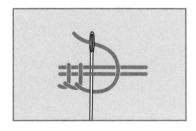

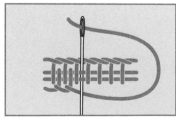

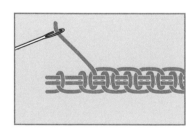

1 Lay two or three long stitches, using a tapestry needle and firm twist thread. Work one pass of well-spaced buttonhole stitch.

2 Turn and work a second row, dovetailing the verticals.

3 A variation made by looping across two verticals.

CRETAN STITCHES

Cretan stitch

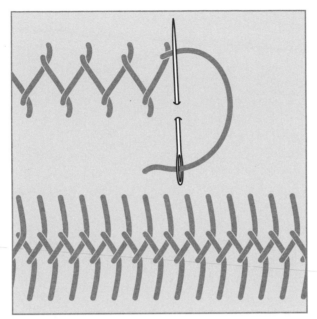

The stitches may be worked wide-spaced (top) or close together (bottom). They make good border stitches as well as fillings. The crossing effect is achieved by keeping the thread on the outside of the needle at every stitch.

Cretan open filling

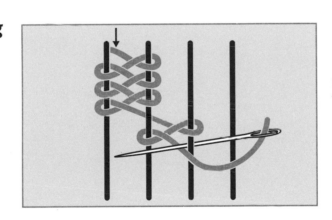

1 Lay a foundation of strong threads. The Cretan stitch is worked without piercing the fabric, except for starting and finishing points.

2 The stitch is worked diagonally in groups of four.

INSERTION STITCH

Faggoting (twisted insertion)

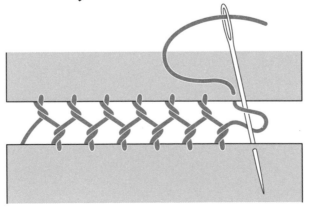

Take the two edges to be joined and lay them parallel to each other before basting both onto strong backing paper. Work from left to right. Bring needle through lower edge and insert into top edge from back to front, a little to the right. Twist needle under and over thread across the gap, then insert into lower edge from back to front, again to the right. Repeat to the end, remove paper.

FILLING STITCHES

Satin (damask) stitch

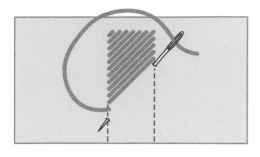

Satin stitch probably originated in China, to complement their beautiful silk threads. Work stitches very closely together to cover fabric completely. Needle in and out at the same angle within a defined outline.

This Chinese swallow design can be worked in sections of satin stitch. For a subtle sheen, try using twisted silk embroidery thread rather than six-stranded cotton [floss]. Arrange the birds in mirrored pairs, or six or seven in a circle.

Long and short satin stitch

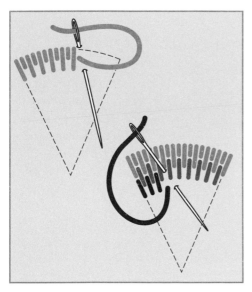

Using a frame, work the first row in alternate, distinctly long and short satin stitches, following your outlined shape (left). Dovetail subsequent rows in equal length stitches (right), using different colors for a shaded effect.

Brick filling

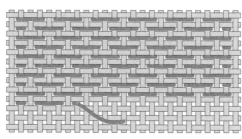

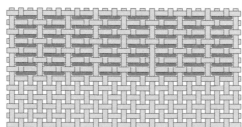

Work back and forth either vertically or horizontally on evenly woven fabric. Edges consist of long and short running stitches (top). Subsequent stitches are of equal length and parallel. Otherwise, arrange running stitch in columns (bottom). Both versions require even tension.

Brick and cross filling

1 Work groups of four satin stitches either vertically or horizontally, allowing equal spaces for the cross stitch.

2 Make sure that all the top stitches of the crosses go in one direction.

Surface darning

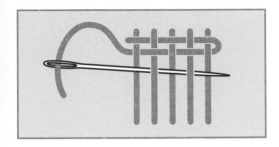

Lay a foundation of vertical threads and, without piercing the fabric except at starting and finishing points, weave top thread back and forth horizontally. If desired, use different colors to create woven patterns.

Trellis couched filling

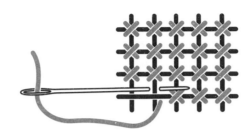

Work a grid of long, evenly spaced straight stitches. In a second color, if desired, bring needle through at each intersection and work a cross stitch. A good filler for blackwork.

Roumanian stitch

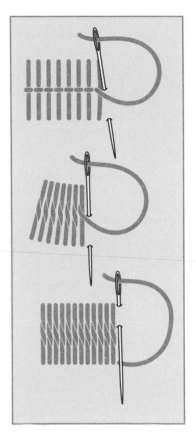

A good substitute for satin stitch and very versatile in terms of spacing and arrangement in blocks, fans and so on. Long vertical stitches are tied down by the next stitch worked across, either horizontal (top) or diagonal.

Cloud filling

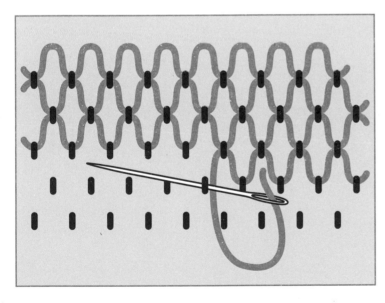

This stitch is best done with twist or pearl thread. Work regular rows of small vertical stitches, alternately spaced. Lace a second color through foundation stitches, without piercing the fabric. Two loops meet under each vertical stitch. Alternatively, lace with narrow ribbon.

Ermine stitch

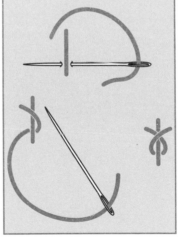

Work long, straight stitch (top) and tie with a cross. Space stitches evenly, with crosses wider at the top than at base.

COUCHING STITCHES

Couching is a technique in which one (heavier) thread is laid on the surface of the fabric and sewn into position by a different (finer) one. It is an economical method that helps rare or costly threads go further since they stay on the surface and are not "wasted" on the wrong side; and if the ground fabric is delicate and the couched threads are heavy, neither is damaged in the process.

Couching stitches

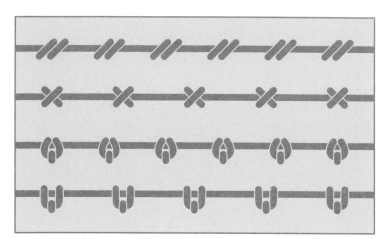

Plain

Cross stitch (p. 18)

Single chain (p. 22)

Fly stitch (p. 21)

Tied cross stitch

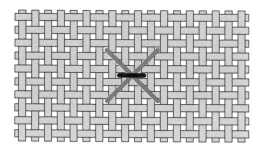

On an evenly woven fabric, work a cross stitch and bring needle through, level with center. Make one straight stitch across center. If desired, do a foundation row of cross stitch, then stitch central ties with a row of running stitch in a second color.

Bokhara

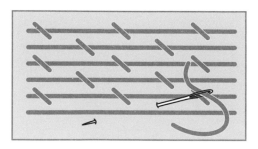

The couched thread should be laid down fairly slack and held by small, evenly spaced stitches, which are pulled tightly over the foundation thread. This is also a simple, rapid way of producing a solid filling, in which case the couching is worked in slanting lines with tying stitches alternately spaced, row by row.

SMOCKING STITCHES

Smocking is a traditional form of hand embroidery, worked over small folds of evenly gathered pre-shrunk fabric (allow three to four times the final width.) When the gathering threads are removed the result is quite stretchy, making it ideal for use on children's clothes. For inclusion in soft furnishings, panels of smocked silk, linen, or velvet look luxurious on cushion [pillow] covers.

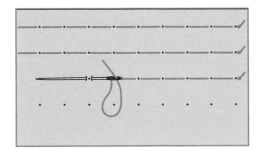

I Unless you are smocking a gingham or stripe, where the pattern provides a guide, you will have to iron a transfer of smocking dots onto the wrong side of your fabric and with the grain. Stitch between the dots as shown, using contrasting thread that will be easy to remove.

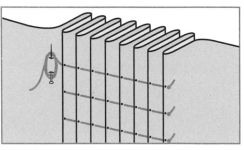

2 Pull up the gathering threads, not too tightly. Tie in pairs or wrap around pins, keeping fabric to the desired width. Make sure gathers are even. Embroider across the fronts of the folds. Use stranded embroidery cotton [floss] but work with only three strands at a time in an embroidery needle (p. 5).

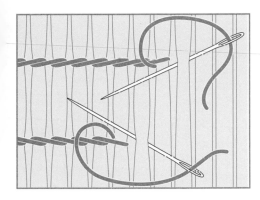

Stem stitch Because smocking is meant to be fairly elastic, try not to work too tightly. Make your first row in this simple stitch to test and establish your tension.

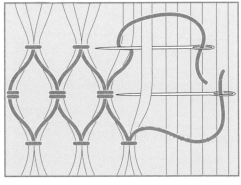

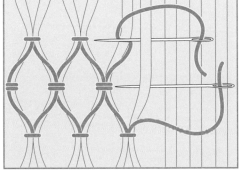

Surface honeycomb A stitch with plenty of stretch. Back stitch across two folds, needle out between them, drop ¼ in [6 mm] and enter next right-hand fold from right to left, back stitch again. Repeat sequence, going up and down alternately. Invert lower line to form honeycomb pattern. Always check thread is correctly above or below needle.

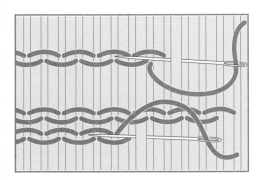

Cable stitch A firm stitch. Needle out through first fold left, thread below needle and stitch over second fold, bringing needle out between first and second. Work with thread above and below needle alternately. Double cable stitch is two rows of cable worked together so they reflect each other.

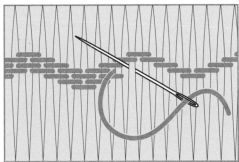

Double closed wave A firm stitch. While making one set of steps upwards, slant the needle up slightly and keep thread below it. On the downward steps, slant the needle down and keep thread above it. A second or third row is made to fit into the zigzags, either close together, as shown, or spaced.

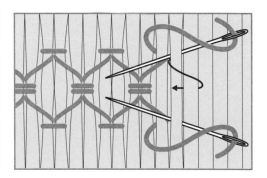

Diamond stitch A large, stretchy stitch that encloses two folds. Needle out on second line, up to first. Back stitch over first fold and then the second with thread above needle. Needle down to second line. Back stitch third fold, then the fourth with thread below. Needle up to fifth fold and repeat. Start second stage on the third line, to complete the shape.

A BACK STITCH ALPHABET

A sampler-style alphabet with matching numerals, designed to be executed in back stitch using just two or three strands of embroidery cotton [floss].

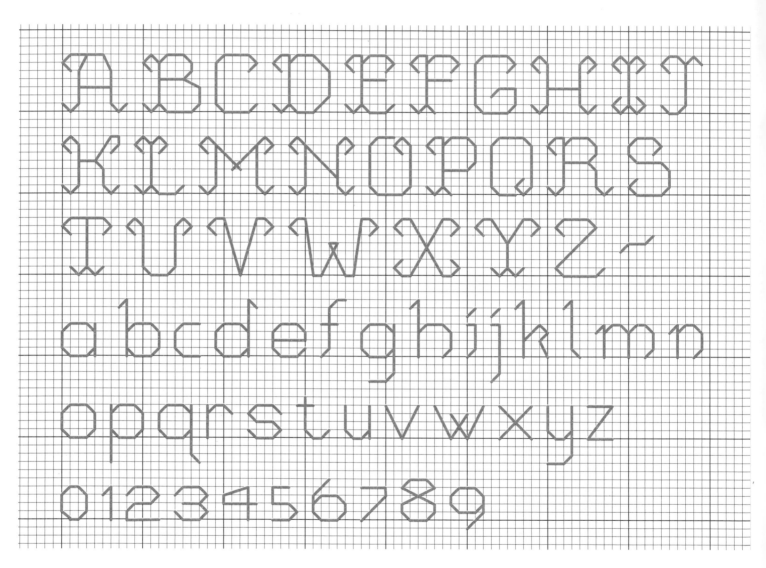

This alphabet is not only for samplers, it is also suitable for lettering embroidered greetings cards or for signing and dating your own projects. Use it as a guide for other stitches when working monograms onto pockets, covered buttons or handkerchiefs, and to personalize gift items such as bookmarks, key fobs, wallets and phone cases.

PART THREE:

MACHINE EMBROIDERY METHODS AND TECHNIQUES

THE SEWING MACHINE

A well-built sewing machine will give years of service so long as it is properly used and maintained.

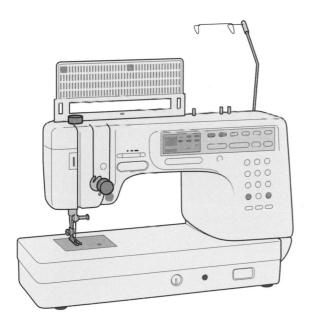

Threading the machine

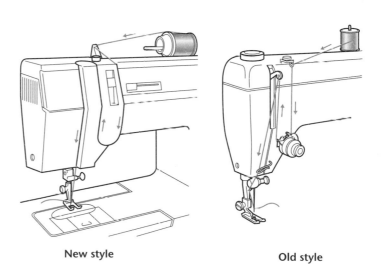

New style   Old style

As a beginner or occasional sewer, look no further than a basic electric model that sews different sizes of straight, hem, stretch and zigzag stitches at the twist of a dial, and a good range of decorative stitches too.

Computerized sewing machines (shown above) are controlled by microchips and several internal motors, making them extremely versatile as well as more expensive. Operated via a touch screen and LCD display, they can memorize and reproduce past tasks and offer hundreds of different stitches, fonts and designs via downloads from a PC.

Newer-style machines incorporate tension disks, thread guides and a take-up lever inside the casing, which eliminates a number of steps involved in threading older models. Consult the manufacturer's manual. If you have no printed instructions, search for your make and model online, where a huge range of manuals is available. Be aware that some needles thread from front to back and some from left to right. Incorrect threading is probably responsible for more beginners' problems than anything else. Always raise the presser foot while threading the machine and lower it when putting it away.

Needle, presser foot, feed-dogs, needle plate

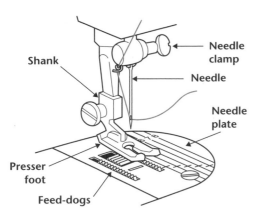

Shank

Needle clamp

Needle

Needle plate

Presser foot

Feed-dogs

Ordinary machine needles are available in sizes 60-130 [8-19]; keep spare sets and change frequently. Avoid bending or breaking them by raising the needle clear before removing work and don't drag while stitching. The finest needle will stitch delicates and the thickest is for tough fabrics like twill. Fit a ballpoint needle for knits or stretch fabrics; use a large-eyed, sharp topstitch needle to take thicker thread and pierce multiple layers.

The presser foot holds the fabric flat against the feed-dogs while the needle makes the stitch. Feed-dogs have tiny metal teeth that move the fabric from front to back as stitching proceeds. The needle plate fits over the feed-dogs, covering the bobbin, with a hole for the tip of the needle to pass through. In free-motion stitching (with or without a presser foot) the feed-dogs are lowered or covered, allowing the fabric to be moved about manually, often while held taut in a hoop.

Five useful machine feet for embroiderers

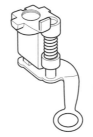

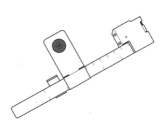

1 Straight-stitch The general purpose presser foot that comes ready to use on most sewing machines.

2 Zigzag Has a horizontal slot for the "swing" of the needle as it forms a zigzag with the thread. Use this foot with multiple needles but do not attempt zigzag stitch with them.

3 Embroidery/ darning Use in free-motion embroidery together with lowered feed-dogs and hooped fabric. Allows maneuvrability of fabric and close control of stitching while protecting the fingers.

4 Walking/quilting Uses teeth to feed upper and lower layers of fabric together evenly and avoid bunching. Also ideal for vinyl, velvets and fabrics that tend to slip or stretch.

5 Circular sewing attachment A sliding attachment fixes the radius with a slotted pin to hold the center of the fabric while a perfect circle is worked in the chosen stitch.

Speciality needles

1 Twin needle Requires two spools of top thread but interlocks with a single bobbin. The effect is two equidistant stitch lines on top and a zigzag beneath. Can be used only where the top threading system is from front to back and the needle plate has a hole wide enough. Triple needles are also available.

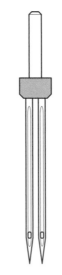

2 Wing needle The blade on each side of the needle pushes open the weave of the fabric where the needle penetrates. Creates decorative effects resembling drawn thread work (see rear cover).

Bobbin

The bobbin holds the lower thread. It lies next to the needle plate, in a compartment with a sliding lid. Fluff [lint] collects here and should be brushed out often. Lower thread tension is controlled by a small screw that regulates the spring on the bobbin case. Certain techniques and types of thread require altered tension. If you use them regularly, keep two or three cases adjusted to different tensions, rather than constantly tightening and loosening the same one.

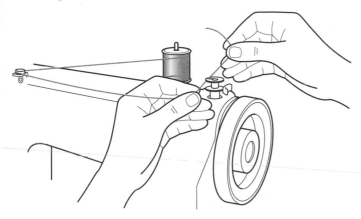

The bobbin is filled automatically from the winder on the machine, which ensures it is evenly wound under tension. Some bobbins can be filled in situ under the plate.

This type sits vertically in the bobbin race and is released by a latch on the case. When replaced, the thread should slot under the spring with a tail of 4 in [10 cm].

The "drop-in" type sits horizontally beneath the plate. There is usually an angled slot to pull the bobbin thread through.

Thread tension

Regular machine stitching is formed by the top and lower threads interlocking in the fabric. Creative machine embroiderers manipulate thread tension for deliberate effects.

1 Top thread tension is governed by the tension dial, numbered 0–9. Behind it, the thread runs between two or three discs that are adjusted according to the dial.

2 Between 4 and 5 on the dial is considered "normal" tension. The threads meet in the center of the fabric and the stitching appears the same on each side.

3 Below 4, the tension discs loosen and the top thread runs more freely. The thread can then pass through both layers of fabric. You can create gathers on a long stitch setting by pulling up the bottom thread.

4 Above 5, the discs are screwed together more tightly and the reverse happens.

Stitch length and width

Stitch length is measured from 1 to 6 and controlled by a dial or lever on the front of the machine. This activates the feed-dogs. Use the longest stitches (⅛-¼ in [4-6 mm]) for heavyweight fabrics, topstitching, gathering and basting. Medium length stitches (3⁄32-⅛ in [2.5-4 mm]) are suitable for mid-weight fabrics. Fine fabrics use a 1⁄16 in [2 mm] stitch. A row of 1⁄32 in [1 mm] stitches is difficult to undo so try to be sure of what you are doing when using the smallest.

Stitch width does not apply to straight stitching. The width control – also found on the front of the machine – sets the "swing" of the needle when working zigzag or other decorative stitches. The measurement usually goes up to ¼ in [6 mm]. For free-motion embroidery, try setting the machine for a wide zigzag and stitch fast to produce a satin effect.

USING HOOPS AND STABILIZERS

The manufacturers of computerized machines supply hoops and frames that move automatically to produce preprogramed patterns. However it is possible to achieve impressive results using only a basic machine and the sprung version of a hand embroidery hoop.

Sprung hoops

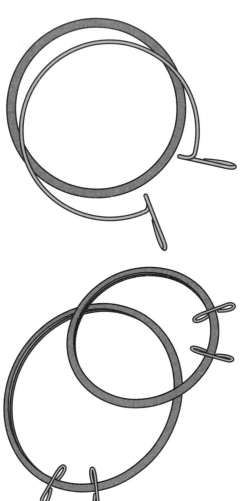

This slim hoop slides under the machine foot and handles well during free-motion stitching. The sprung clip fits on the inside of the hoop and holds the fabric really taut. It is quick and easy to change projects or to move the hoop around a large fabric area.

It is worth pointing out that the traditional wooden hoop also works with machine embroidery, the only difference being that the rim is turned upward so that the wrong side of the fabric rests flat against the base plate.

You can avoid hoop marks on your fabric by fixing a sheet of one-sided adhesive stabilizer tightly into the hoop itself. Peel off the backing within the hoop and stick the fabric flat to the stabilizer. Densely stitched designs will require a heavy support to ensure the work doesn't pucker, while lighter pieces should not be made too stiff.

Stabilizers

Stabilizers are used above or below the fabric – with or without a hoop – to prevent it shifting or stretching while machining. There are various kinds, from paper, cotton and open mesh to nylon and polyvinyl alcohol. The "tear away" or "cut away" sort is removed once the stitching is complete, retained only on the back of the stitched area itself. This type is frequently used for T-shirts, knits and synthetic fabrics. Another type is a smooth non-woven cotton stabilizer, available plain or as an "iron-on" for stretch fabrics.

There is an easy-tear, cold-water soluble stabilizer designed for fleeces and lightweight delicates. There is also a heavyweight version, ideal for complex free-motion embroidery and – when used without any base fabric at all – it offers embroiderers the exciting chance to produce pure lace or filigree work.

For any project that cannot be wetted or is too delicate to withstand tearing, choose the heat-sensitive vanishing muslin that obligingly disintegrates under a dry iron or in a moderate oven and can be brushed away. Finally, there is a hot-water soluble fabric that can be three-dimensionally molded if sufficient residue is allowed to remain after boiling.

TECHNIQUES TO TRY

Practicing a technique or element of design encourages you to develop your ideas instead of rigidly following a pattern. Experiment with the threads and fabric you want to use – glossy, matt or metallic – as your choice can alter the whole look and purpose of a piece.

Regular pattern

Work wide zigzag stitch in short parallel lines vertically and horizontally. Try this on coarse canvas and then velvet – the results will be very different.

Uneven tension

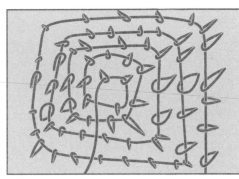

Work a straight-stitched spiral with the top thread tension too tight and the bottom too loose. Try different colors for the top thread and bobbin.

Textures

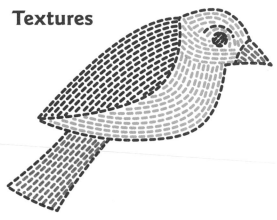

Fill areas with regular rows of straight stitch in different threads and colors. Needle down at the end of a row, raise the foot and turn the fabric through 180 degrees before lowering the foot again.

Filling patterns

Sashiko A filling pattern carried out in long, straight stitch. Use a white twist thread on a dark fabric to echo Japanese Sashiko style.

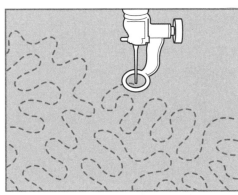

Free motion machining in straight stitch with an embroidery/darning foot and the feed-dogs lowered. Stitch fast but move the hoop slowly and smoothly with both hands. Jerky movements make uneven stitches.

Decorated initials

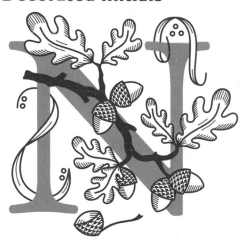

A formal satin-stitched initial superimposed with freestyle decoration. Create twigs from cord made by zigzagging over a core of string or yarn, pulled steadily through the machine.

TWO SPECIAL EFFECTS

Cutwork and appliqué are two stitching techniques that can be done by either hand or machine. The latter can save time on a large project.

CUTWORK

Machine eyelet border

Eyelet, whitework and broderie anglaise are all variations of cutwork and look best stitched in glossy thread on a matt cotton base. A pattern is marked out on the fabric and defined with two lines of straight stitch plus one more line run between them for "padding" before embroidery begins.

Eyelet embroidery foot

The embroidery is worked around a punched hole in a close zigzag or satin stitch. Vertical spring action of the foot stops the fabric lifting with the needle and gives consistent stitching, even at speed.

Cutwork

Turn to WS and cut the fabric off as close as possible to the base of the buttonhole stitch.

The smallest eyelets are made with scissor points. One round of stay stitch is followed by buttonhole pulled firmly away from the center, or simply oversewing to neaten the edge.

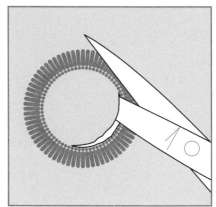

APPLIQUÉ

Appliqué foot

The toes on this foot are shorter than the usual zigzag foot, for smoother stitching and greater maneuvrability. It is particularly suited for satin stitching, appliqué and couching.

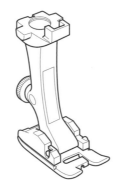

Machine stitched appliqué

It is hard to sew appliqué down flat without a margin. Draw the final outline on the chosen fabric, cut it out with a normal seam allowance and baste to the background. Machine along the drawn line with a straight stitch and cut off excess fabric as close as possible to the stitched line. With even tension top and bottom, set to zigzag around the shape. Stitch fast to produce a satin stitch but move the fabric slowly so the stitching is controlled and covers the raw edges.

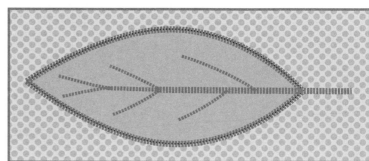

MOTIFS

Here are a few motifs suitable for adaptation to machine embroidery. Try stitching the spirals free-motion in a hoop and see how you can expand them into intricate filling patterns. The solid shapes can also be scaled up (p. 11) for appliqué work.

PROJECT: BAG KEEPER

Keep plastic bags tidy and ready to reuse in this neat bag keeper.

Materials
- Fabric for the embroidered label, cut to any size or shape you wish. With thick felt you probably won't need backing, otherwise cut iron-on Vilene or stabilizer to fit
- Cotton fabric for the bag itself, 20 x 25 in [51 x 63.5 cm]
- Elastic ¼ in [7 mm] wide, cut into two lengths, 12 in [30 cm] and 6 in [15 cm]
- Ribbon or tape for the handle, 15 in [37.5 cm] long, ¾ in [20 mm] wide
- You will also need a sewing machine, needles, threads, bodkin, scissors and an iron

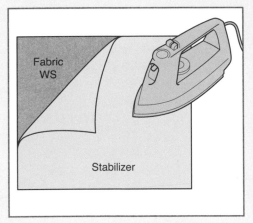

Fabric WS

Stabilizer

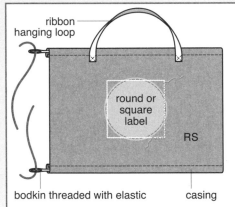

ribbon
hanging loop

round or square label

RS

bodkin threaded with elastic   casing

1 Attach the Vilene or stabilizer to the label fabric. The elephant image can be squared up for either embroidery or appliqué. You might like to trace your own handwriting on embroiderer's carbon paper, or copy the alphabet (p. 30). If you prefer hand embroidery, you could make the elephant into a sampler of your favorite stitches or stitch it in a regional style. In that case, hoop the fabric for embroidering and interface with Vilene only when finished.

2 Take the bag fabric and make a ½ in [13 mm] casing on both long sides by first folding over ¾ in [20 mm] and then turning the raw edge under again by ¼ in [7 mm]. Baste the turning and machine stitch the casings, close to the fold.

3 Measure and pin your label to the center. Attach it with a decorative machine stitch or plain topstitch. Fold in the raw ends of the ribbon and sew the handle firmly near the top edge, about 7 in [17.5 cm] from either end and below the casing.

4 With the bodkin, run the 12 in [30 cm] elastic through the top casing, gathering fabric as you go. Sew down the ends close to each edge. Repeat with the bottom casing, using the 6 in [15 cm] elastic. The opening at the bottom is narrower than the top.

5 Fold the bag in half lengthways, wrong side out. With a ½ in [13 mm] seam allowance, machine the side seam from top to bottom, ensuring that the ends of the elastic are firmly included. Press the seam smooth if necessary.

WS

6 Turn the bag right side out and hang up ready for use.

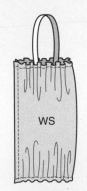

PART FOUR:
REGIONAL EMBROIDERY

THE INDIAN TRADITION

From a prime position on land and maritime trade routes between China and Europe, India has gathered a rich tradition of embroidery, especially in the northwest border region of Gujarat.

Printing blocks

The carrier of many Indian patterns and motifs is the simple hand-carved wooden printing block. More precise geometric patterns are printed from metal strips, hammered edge-on into the face of the wood. Both kinds are stamped onto the base fabric as a stitching guide.

Aari work

Chain stitch is worked in frames large and small (fabric tightly stretched and right side up) using either a needle or a small hooked awl called an aari, similar to the western tambour hook. With the thread held beneath the fabric, the hook is inserted downward (a) and the thread caught, the hook turned and drawn upward in a loop. With the hook above the fabric (b) and light tension on the lower thread, it is turned and inserted again at a short distance and another loop is drawn up through the center of the previous one. With each action of the aari, the embroiderer twists it vertically through 180 degrees to hold the thread. Cotton, silk, and wool are all used in aari work (see rear cover for an antique silk example from Gujarat, c. 1760).

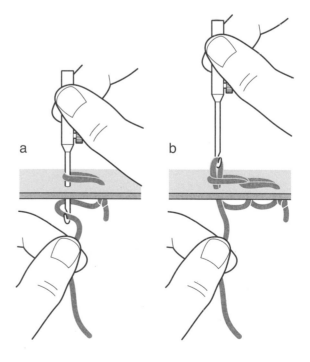

Shisha mirror work

Small, round, factory-made mirrors are the
most commonly used; large sequins are
an unbreakable alternative. Attach with
a choice of stitches: buttonhole (p. 24),
herringbone (p. 20), twisted chain (p. 40)
or Cretan (p. 25) or for a more elaborate
effect, a combination of several. Slipped
chain (p. 23) is frequently used last as a
radiating outline.

Anchor the mirror to the fabric with two
horizontal and two vertical stitches (a)
and (b). Pass the needle under the first
intersection, cross over and make a stitch

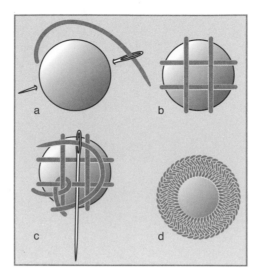

from right to left (c). With even tension as you go, continue counterclockwise until the
frame is complete (d). An alternative method is to wrap a small ring with colored thread,
place it over the mirror and slip stitch firmly into place.

Twisted chain

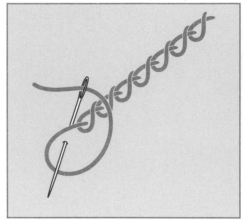

A chain variation that gives a raised line and
makes a useful addition to the texture of a
Shisha surround.

Badla

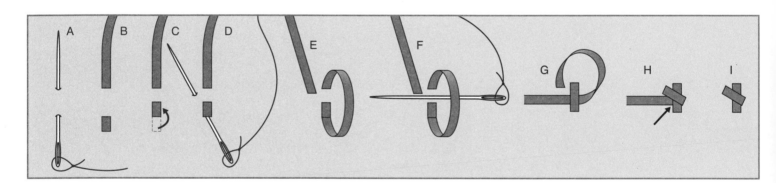

A metal embroidery technique that consists of producing tiny dots
(fardi), and also very small eyelets and sequins that twinkle like
stars on fine translucent materials such as voile, muslin and silk.
The "thread" is narrow strips of recycled metal approximately
$\frac{1}{16}$ in [2 mm] wide and 12 in [30 cm] long.

Working in the hand, the special badla needle is threaded (A) and
the metal pulled through the ground fabric until a short tail is
left. This is bent over to secure it (B and C). The needle is inserted
again (D) and pulled through to make a loop (E). It is then passed
through the loop (F) and the metal strip forms a cross (G). The
strip is pulled flush to the fabric and broken off (H). The fardi is
complete (I). The Badla is finally burnished with a smooth stone.

Banjara

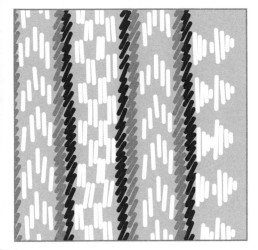

Banjara is the name given to the nomadic tribes of India. Their close-stitched, colorful, cotton-on-cotton embroidery is arranged in solid geometric patterns, making extensive use of straight and Florentine-style stitchwork.

Kantha

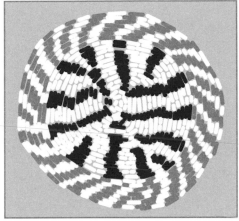

Kantha, meaning "rags," is a style of cotton quilting from Bengal. Running stitch provides the basis combined with back, stem and split stitches, and pattern darning, to work a series of characteristic motifs.

Kutch cross stitch

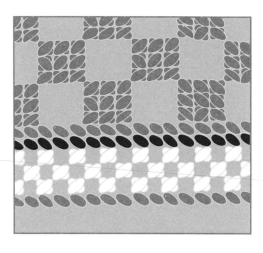

Minute cross stitch of such precision that it almost appears woven. This work is easier carried out by the counted thread method on an evenly woven fabric

Shadow work with closed herringbone

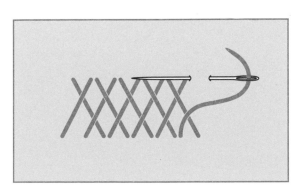

Shadow work is an element of the Indian whitework technique called Chikan. Worked on the wrong side of transparent fabrics such as voile and organza, the closed herringbone produces two lines of back stitch on the front.

Double back stitch (shadow work)

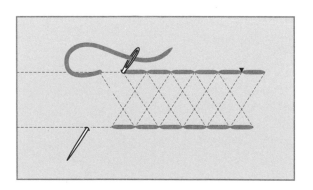

The back stitch on the right side of shadow work forms a continuous outline to the herringbone filling. The crosses show through the fabric, creating a distinct tonal variation.

PROJECT: PEACOCK CUSHION COVER

The cushion cover is assembled from recycled pieces of block-printed cotton and silk, appliquéd with an embroidered peacock motif. Printed fabrics always add character and speak of the time and part of the world they belong to, see a similar project shown on the rear cover.

Select fabrics of matching weight, choosing colors and prints that coordinate with one another. Iron well before cutting out each patch; include a ½ in [13mm] seam allowance.

Right sides facing, machine stitch the pieces together in blocks as shown below. Once finished, press seams on the wrong side.

Scale up (p. 11), draw and cut the peacock shape from a bright, contrasting fabric; keep a margin of ½ in [13mm].

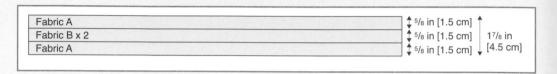

Fabric A	⁵/₈ in [1.5 cm]
Fabric B x 2	⁵/₈ in [1.5 cm]
Fabric A	⁵/₈ in [1.5 cm]

1⁷/₈ in [4.5 cm]

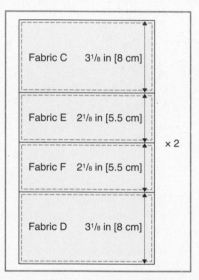

Fabric C	3¹/₈ in [8 cm]
Fabric E	2¹/₈ in [5.5 cm]
Fabric F	2¹/₈ in [5.5 cm]
Fabric D	3¹/₈ in [8 cm]

× 2

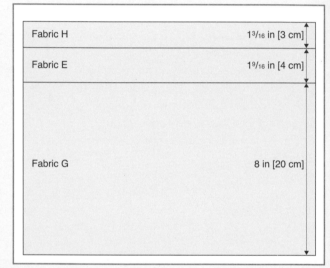

Fabric H	1³/₁₆ in [3 cm]
Fabric E	1⁹/₁₆ in [4 cm]
Fabric G	8 in [20 cm]

Attach the motif to the right side of the patchwork by hand with rows of running stitch in brightly colored embroidery threads. Finally, outline with chain stitch.

Trim off the extra fabric close to the chain stitch. Draw on the tail feathers with a soluble marker. Fill them in using herringbone stitch in various colors and outline again with a contrasting chain stitch.

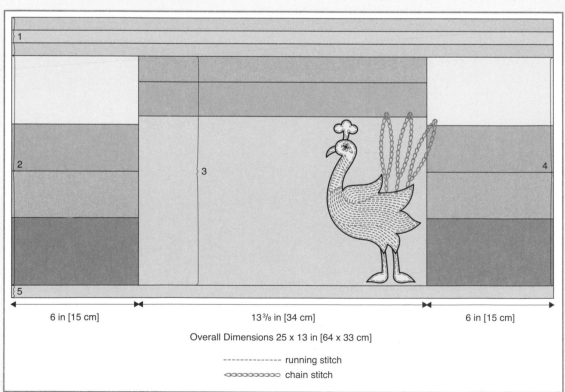

6 in [15 cm]   13³/₈ in [34 cm]   6 in [15 cm]

Overall Dimensions 25 x 13 in [64 x 33 cm]

- - - - - - - - running stitch
⋘⋘⋘⋘⋘ chain stitch

THE PERUVIAN PARACAS

Some amazing 2,000-year-old textiles came to light in the 1920s with the discovery of a vast necropolis on the Paracas peninsula. Each mummified body was ritually wrapped in layers of ornate embroideries (see rear cover).

Peruvian cat in stem stitch

The parading beasts, birds and strange flying figures (right and below) were meticulously worked in sections of close stem stitch, covering the cotton base weave at different angles and lengths (see below right). The alpaca wool threads took the dyes well, so the array of purples, deep reds, pinks, yellows, and greens remain vivid even now.

Flying figures

Monkey

Stem stitch formation

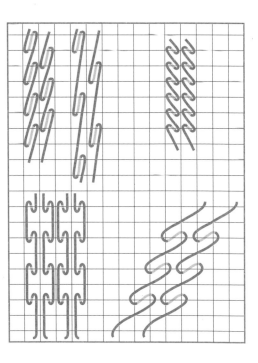

EUROPEAN FOLK EMBROIDERY

European embroidery has typically looked to linen and wool for everyday use, with most of the exquisite gold and silk examples reserved for the Church.

Russian cross stitch

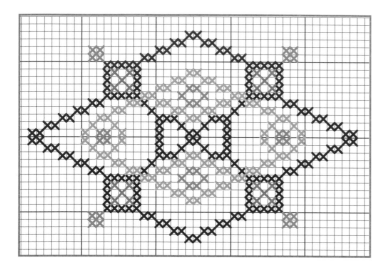

This four-color motif was chosen to decorate a plain white glazed cotton apron. The grid pattern (above left) shows how the design is plotted for stitching over waste canvas. The canvas is basted onto the cotton fabric and the cross stitch is worked through both layers simultaneously. When finished, the threads of the waste canvas are cut and withdrawn to leave the design intact on the plain ground (above right).

Hungarian "written" embroidery

This is a much-enlarged section of a convoluted double chain-stitch pattern, worked in red twist on a white linen bag. The pattern is from Kalotaszeg in Transylvania, once part of Hungary. This traditional style is called "written" embroidery, designed by the local Writing Woman, who memorizes hundreds of patterns and can draw them freehand, to order, on blank linen. Stylized floral motifs predominate and the stitch used is always one of the chain family, such as broad chain (p. 22), open chain (p. 22) or heavy chain (braid) stitch.

The bag itself is stitched together with blanket stitch in matching thread.

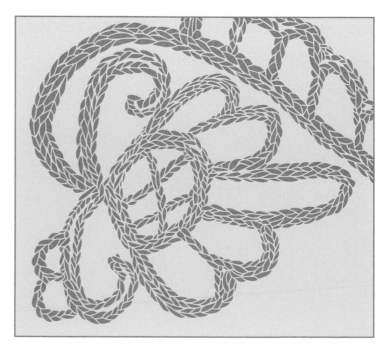

Apart from the nobility and town dwellers, for centuries most Europeans worked on the land. They also sewed their own clothes and household linen, which naturally led to decorating them too, usually with motifs and colors specific to their own communities. Existence was hard and nothing was allowed to go to waste. They would embroider only the parts of a garment that showed, like collars, sleeves, and hems. Counted thread embroidery – chiefly cross stitch – is found everywhere from the "dixos" (medallions) of the Greek islands to Scandinavia. Chain, stem, split and Cretan stitches gave embroiderers greater scope to create more flowing outlines and complex fillings.

Icelandic cross stitch

Crowned heart design.

Romanian chain and satin stitch

The sleeve motif from a folk costume.

Chinese satin stitch

Satin-weave fabric (p. 8) and satin stitch embroidery (p. 26) have long been used by the Chinese to show off the sheer beauty of their silk threads. The tomb of an aristocratic woman who died in 1243 CE yielded fabulous gold satin embroideries of flowering branches and perching birds. However, satin stitch had displaced chain stitch even earlier, in the Tang era (618–906 CE). And later, during the trading boom of the eighteenth and nineteenth centuries, most of the silk that China exported to the West was patterned with satin embroidery because such delicate designs were quicker and easier to produce by hand than via the complexities of loom weaving.

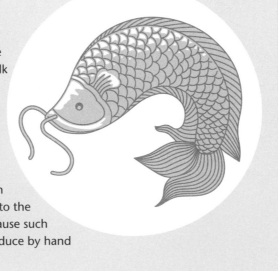

WASHING AND MOUNTING

Washing embroidery

Most contemporary embroidery threads are colorfast, but if you have any doubts, press a damp cotton pad against the stitching (preferably on the wrong side). If it stains the cotton pad, the embroidery should be dry cleaned. Wash colorfast pieces in lukewarm water only with pure soap flakes. Squeeze gently and do not rub the stitching. Rinse in several changes of cool water before rolling the embroidery in a clean towel to remove excess water. Unwrap and gently pull the piece into shape. Dry away from direct heat or strong sunlight. If the piece has become distorted, "block" it by stretching and pinning onto a soft board with long, rustproof pins around the edge. Leave until totally dry. Always iron face down on a padded surface, using a damp pressing cloth if necessary.

Mounting

Cut a mount from thin hardboard, mount board or foam board. Hardboard needs to be sawn but use a sharp craft knife for the others, together with a metal ruler and a cutting mat. Keep your fingers behind the cutting edge. To pad your work for display, cut the batting to the exact size of the mount board. When using hardboard, mount the fabric against the rough side.

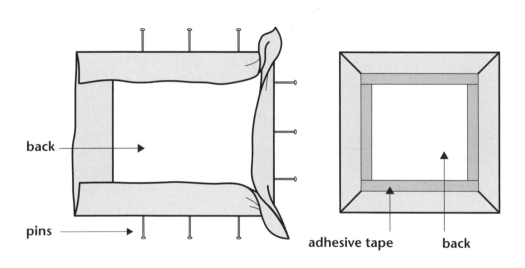

back

pins

adhesive tape

back

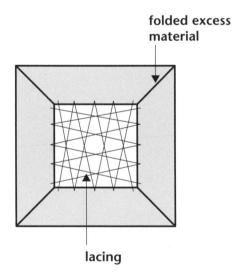

folded excess material

lacing

1 Lay the piece face down and place the mount board on top with the batting in between. Fold the fabric up and pin to the edges of the board. Turn and check for positioning (you may need to re-pin a few times). Ensure the edges of the board align with the weave of the fabric.

2 Hardboard will not take pins so use adhesive tape for positioning. If you don't want any lacing, fold the corners neatly, pull the fabric taut and tape the fabric foldover to the back of the board all round. Be aware that any adhesive tape eventually deteriorates; never use on or near the embroidered area.

3 Fold the fabric corners neatly and start lacing across the back from the middle of one of the shorter sides. Use a strong thread and work a giant herringbone stitch (p. 20) from side to side to avoid straining on a single hole in the fabric. Keep the thread tight enough to pull the surface taut without distorting the embroidery. Repeat across the two remaining sides.

GLOSSARY

Aari a small hooked awl used in Indian embroidery, similar to the western tambour hook

Aida block weave foundation fabric with regular construction and visible stitch holes

Appliqué decoration cut from one piece of fabric and stitched to another

Assisi thirteenth-century embroidery technique from the Italian town of the same name

Basting preliminary stitching, removed when work is finished

Batting filling material used as insulation or to pad mounted fabric

Bias lies along any diagonal line between the lengthwise and crosswise grains

Blackwork sixteenth-century embroidery worked in black thread on white linen

Blending filament fine metallic thread for combining with ordinary stranded cotton

Blocking stretching and pinning a fabric to shape

Border decorative frame stitched around a design

Chart grid-type guide to stitch placement in counted-thread embroidery

Couching a thick thread or group of threads sewn down with a thinner thread

Count number of threads per 1 in [2.5 cm] in a foundation fabric

Crewel work wool embroidery on linen, popular for furnishings in the seventeenth century

Digitize conversion of an image to a format that the embroidery machine can interpret

Evenweave foundation fabric with the same number of threads per 1 in [2.5 cm] counted vertically and horizontally

Filling series of stitches used to cover the area within an outline

Finishing trimming threads, removing excess backing, pressing and so on after embroidery is complete

Florentine style counted thread embroidery worked vertically in straight stitch

Frame a four-sided structure that holds fabric taut during embroidery

Freestyle embroidery hand embroidery stitches not linked with the counted-thread technique

Free motion (free machine) technique of machine stitching with free movement of fabric and stabilizer secured in a hoop

Grain the direction in which the warp and weft threads of a fabric lie

Hoop (tambour) an inner and outer ring of wood or plastic tightened together to hold fabric taut during embroidery

Hooping technique of setting up and using an embroidery hoop for machine embroidery

Interfacing non-woven textile that adds body to fabric, either sew-in or iron-on (fusible)

Jump stitch a stitch taken to "jump" across a join or from one part of a design to another

Lark's head knot (loop start) technique for securing thread at the start of work

Monogram embroidered initials

Motif a distinctive design element

Perforated paper lightweight card with regularly spaced holes imitating embroidery canvas

Perle (pearl) shiny twisted embroidery thread, non-divisible

Powdering a single stitch repeated at random across the surface of the fabric

RS the right side or "face" of the fabric

Sampler a decorative display of a variety of embroidery stitches

Scaling proportional enlargement or reduction of a design

Seam allowance distance between the cut edge of the fabric and the seam line

Selvage the solid edge of a woven textile

Space-dyed threads factory-dyed in multiple colors, or in shades of a single color at regular intervals

Stabilizer helps prevent fabric from shifting or stretching during stitching

Stay stitching a line of straight stitches to prevent a curved edge stretching out of shape

Stranded divisible embroidery cotton [floss]

Tacking tambour *see Hoop*

Tweeding Working with different-colored strands in the same needle.

Variegated *see Space-dyed*

Vilene *see Interfacing*

WS the wrong side of the fabric

Wadding warp threads running lengthwise in a woven fabric, parallel to the selvage

Waste knot starting knot placed on RS of fabric and later cut off

Weft threads running crosswise in a woven fabric, at right-angles to the selvage

Z-twist threads spun clockwise

INDEX OF STITCHES

Algerian eye **19**
Arrowhead **18**
Back **16**
Back-stitched chain **23**
Blanket **24**
Bokhara **28**
Bosnian **16**
Boxed cross **19**
Braided cross **19**
Brick filling **26**
Brick and cross filling **26**
Broad chain **22**
Bullion knot **15**
Buttonhole **24**
Buttonhole ring **24**
Buttonhole wheel **24**
Cable smocking **29**
Chain **22**
Checkered chain **22**
Cloud filling **27**
Coral **24**
Coral zigzag **23**
Couching **28**
Cretan **25**
Cretan close-spaced **25**
Cross **19**
Cross stitch couching **28**
Daisy **22**
Detached chain **22**
Diamond stitch **29**

Dog-tooth **16**
Double buttonholed bar **24**
Double closed wave smocking **29**
Double cross **19**
Double feather **21**
Double running **16**
Double running steps **16**
Double threaded back **17**
Ermine filling **27**
Faggoting **25**
Feather **21**
Fern **18**
Filling **26–7**
Fishbone **18**
Fly **21**
Fly couching **28**
Four-legged knot **15**
French knot **15**
Herringbone **20**
Holbein **16**
Insertion **25**
Knotted **15**
Long-armed cross **20**
Long and short satin **26**
Open chain **22**
Pekinese **17**
Raised band chain **23**
Raised band stem **21**
Rice **20**
Roumanian filling **27**

Running **16**
Satin **26**
Scroll **24**
Sheaf **18**
Shisha **40**
Slipped chain **23**
Smocking **29**
Smyrna **19**
Speckling **18**
Split **21**
Stem **21, 43**
Stem stitch smocking **29**
Surface darning filling **27**
Surface honeycomb smocking **29**
Tête de boeuf **22**
Threaded herringbone **20**
Threaded running **17**
Tied cross **28**
Tied herringbone **20**
Trellis back **17**
Trellis couched filling **27**
Twisted chain **40**
Twisted insertion **25**
Wheatear **23**
Whipped chain **23**
Whipped running **17**
Woven cross **19**